# Easy Striped Dishcloth

## Skill Level

 BEGINNER

## Finished Size

8½ inches x 8½ inches

## Materials

- Peaches & Crème medium (worsted) weight cotton yarn (2½ oz/120 yds/71g per ball):
  1 ball each #01730 bright aqua (A) and #01612 sunshine (B)
- H/8/5mm crochet hook or size needed to obtain gauge
- Tapestry needle

## Gauge

13 sc = 4 inches; 11 rows in pattern = 4 inches

Take time to check gauge.

## Pattern Notes

Weave in ends as work progresses.

To change color, work last stitch of row until 2 loops remain on hook, drop working color, do not cut, yarn over with new color and draw through loops on hook. Turn and continue working with new color.

Chain-3 at beginning of row counts as a double crochet unless otherwise stated.

Join with slip stitch as indicated unless otherwise stated.

## Dishcloth

**Row 1 (RS):** With A, ch 26, sc in 2nd ch from hook, sc in each rem ch across, turn. (25 sc)

**Row 2:** Ch 1, sc in each sc across, **changing color to B in last sc** (see Pattern Notes), turn.

**Row 3:** Ch 2 *(does not count as a st)*, hdc in first sc and in each rem sc across, turn.

**Row 4:** Ch 2, hdc in each st across, changing color to A in last sc, turn. (25 hdc)

**Row 5: Ch 3** *(see Pattern Notes)*, dc in each hdc across, turn. (25 dc)

**Row 6:** Ch 3, dc in each dc across, changing color to B in last st, turn. (25 dc)

**Row 7:** Ch 1, sc in each dc across, turn. (25 sc)

**Row 8:** Ch 1, sc in each sc across, changing color to A in last sc, turn.

**Rows 9–20:** [Rep rows 3–8] twice. At end of row 20, do not change color. Fasten off.

## Edging

**Rnd 1 (RS):** With RS facing, join A with sc in last sc of row 20 in left-hand corner, 2 sc in same sc, working across next side in ends of rows, sc in end of each sc and hdc row and 2 sc in end of each dc row across to row 1, sk row 1, working across next side in unused lps of foundation ch, 3 sc in first ch, sc in each ch across to last ch, 3 sc in last ch, working across next side in ends of rows, sk row 1, sc in end of each sc and hdc row and 2 sc in end of each dc row across to row 20, sk end of row 20, working across row 20, 3 sc in first sc, sc in each sc across to first sc, **join** *(see Pattern Notes)* in first sc. (108 sc)

**Rnd 2:** Ch 1, *(sc, ch 2, sc) in next sc, sk next sc, rep from * around, join in first sc. Fasten off. Weave in ends with tapestry needle. ●

**STITCH KEY**
- ○ Chain (ch)
- + Single crochet (sc)
- • Slip stitch (sl st)
- ⊤ Half double crochet (hdc)
- ⊤ Double crochet (dc)

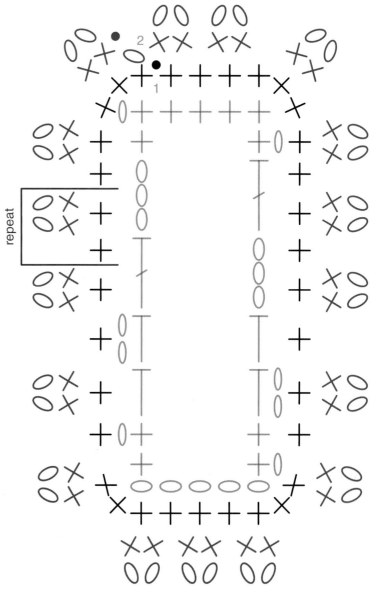

**Easy Striped Dishcloth**
Edging

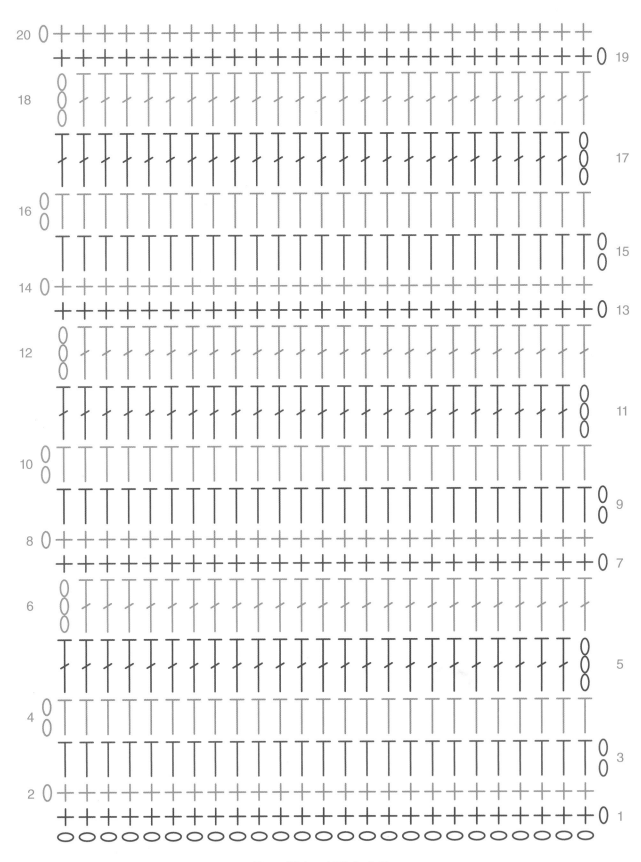

**Easy Striped Dishcloth**
Symbol Diagram

# Pamper Yourself Spa Cloth

## Skill Level
 BEGINNER

## Finished Size
8 inches in diameter

## Materials

- Cascade Ultra Pima light (light worsted) weight yarn (3½ oz/220 yds/100g per skein):
    1 skein #3718 natural
- F/5/3.75mm crochet hook or size needed to obtain gauge
- Locking stitch markers:
    1 in first color
    5 in 2nd color
- Tapestry needle

## Gauge
Rnds 1–12 = 4 inches

Take time to check gauge.

## Pattern Notes
Weave in ends as work progresses.

Join with slip stitch as indicated unless otherwise stated.

All rounds are worked on right side without turning.

## Spa Cloth
**Rnd 1 (RS):** Ch 4, **join** (see Pattern Notes) in first ch to form ring, ch 1, 6 sc in ring, join in first sc. (6 sc)

**Rnd 2:** Ch 1, 2 sc in each sc around, join in first sc. (12 sc)

**Rnd 3:** Ch 1, sc in same sc as joining, 2 sc in next sc, (sc in next sc, 2 sc in next sc) 5 times, join in first sc. (18 sc)

**Rnd 4:** Ch 1, sc in same sc as joining and in next sc, 2 sc in next sc (inc made), [sc in each of next 2 sc, 2 sc in next sc (inc made)] 5 times, join in first sc. (24 sc)

**Rnd 5:** Ch 1, sc in first sc, sc in each sc to 2nd sc of next inc, 2 sc in 2nd sc, [sc in each sc to 2nd sc of next inc, 2 sc in 2nd sc] 5 times, join in first sc. (30 sc)

**Rnds 6–22:** Rep rnd 5. (132 sc at end of rnd 22)

**Rnd 23:** Ch 1, [sl st in next sc, ch 1] around, join in first st. Fasten off.

## Flower

**Rnd 1:** Ch 4, join in first ch to form ring, ch 1, 6 sc in ring, join in first sc. *(6 sc)*

**Rnd 2:** Ch 1, 2 sc in each sc around, join in first sc. *(12 sc)*

**Rnds 3–6:** Rep rnd 2. At end of last rnd, fasten off, leaving 8-inch tail. *(192 sc at end of rnd 6)*

## Finishing

With tapestry needle and yarn tail, sew Flower to center of Spa Cloth. ●

**STITCH KEY**
○ Chain (ch)
+ Single crochet (sc)
• Slip stitch (sl st)

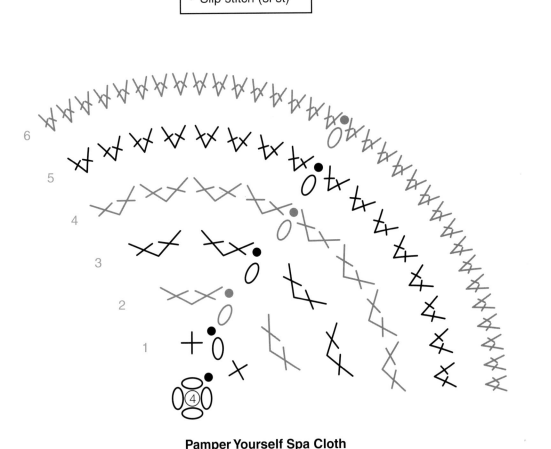

**Pamper Yourself Spa Cloth**
Flower

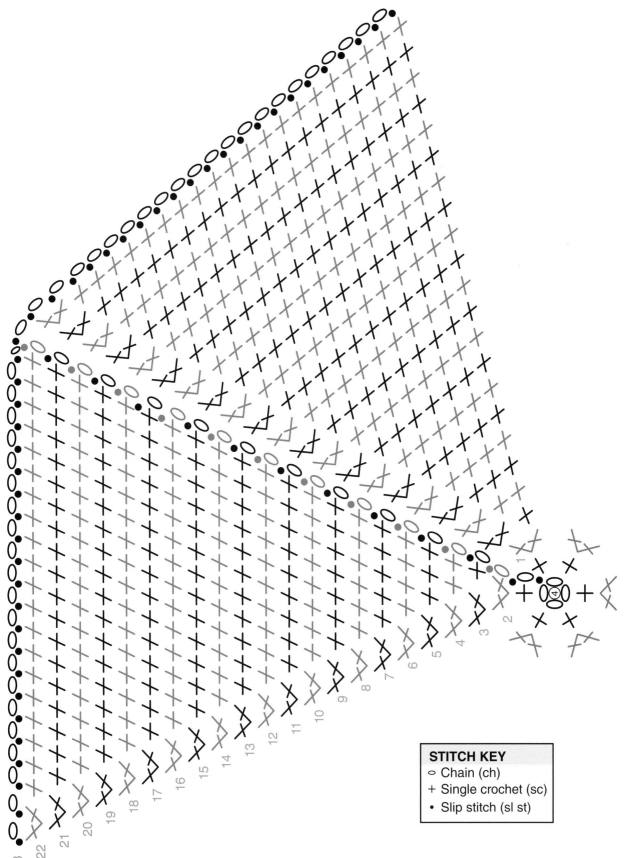

**Pamper Yourself Spa Cloth**
Symbol Diagram

**STITCH KEY**
∘ Chain (ch)
+ Single crochet (sc)
• Slip stitch (sl st)

# Sweet & Sassy Hats

## Skill Level
 EASY

## Finished Size
16 (19, 22) inches in circumference

## Materials
- Medium (worsted) weight yarn (3 oz/185 yds/85g per ball):
  - 1 (1, 1) ball light aqua or
  - 1 (1, 1) ball light gray
- H/8/5mm crochet hook or size needed to obtain gauge
- Tapestry needle
- Stitch marker

## Gauge
16 sc = 4 inches; 20 rows in pattern = 4 inches

Rnds 1–6 = 3 inches

Take time to check gauge.

## Special Stitches
**Cluster (cl):** Holding back last lp of each st on hook, 3 dc in indicated st, yo and draw through all 4 lps on hook.

**Double crochet decrease (dc dec):** (Yo, insert hook in indicated st, yo, draw lp through, yo, draw through 2 lps on hook) twice, yo and draw through all 3 lps on hook.

**Joined double crochet decrease (joined dc dec):** Yo, insert hook in indicated st, yo, draw lp through, yo, draw through 2 lps on hook, insert hook in top 2 lps of 3rd ch of beg ch-5, yo, draw through both lps and 2 lps on hook.

**Picot:** Ch 3, hdc in 3rd ch from hook.

## Pattern Notes

Weave in ends as work progresses.

Join with slip stitch as indicated unless otherwise stated.

All rounds are worked on the right side without turning.

Hat is worked in a continuous spiral without joining.

Place marker in first stitch of each round and move up as work progresses.

Chain-5 at beginning of round counts as a treble crochet and a chain-1 space.

## Hat

**Rnd 1:** Ch 4, **join** *(see Pattern Notes)* in first ch to form ring, ch 1, 6 sc in ring. *(6 sc)*

**Rnd 2:** 2 sc in each sc. *(12 sc)*

**Rnd 3:** (Sc in next sc, 2 sc in next sc) 6 times. *(18 sc)*

**Rnd 4:** (Sc in each of next 2 sc, 2 sc in next sc) 6 times. *(24 sc)*

**Rnd 5:** (Sc in each of next 3 sc, 2 sc in next sc) 6 times. *(30 sc)*

**Rnd 6:** (Sc in each of next 4 sc, 2 sc in next sc) 6 times. *(36 sc)*

**Rnd 7:** (Sc in each of next 5 sc, 2 sc in next sc) 6 times. *(42 sc)*

**Rnd 8:** (Sc in each of next 6 sc, 2 sc in next sc) 6 times. *(48 sc)*

**Rnd 9:** (Sc in each of next 7 sc, 2 sc in next sc) 6 times. *(54 sc)*

**Rnd 10:** (Sc in each of next 8 sc, 2 sc in next sc) 6 times. *(60 sc)*

**Rnd 11:** (Sc in each of next 9 sc, 2 sc in next sc) 6 times. *(66 sc)*

## Size 16-Inch Hat
Continue with All Sizes.

## Size 19-Inch & 22-Inch Hats
**Rnd 12:** (Sc in each of next 10 sc, 2 sc in next sc) 6 times. *(72 sc)*

**Rnd 13:** (Sc in each of next 11 sc, 2 sc in next sc) 6 times. *(78 sc)*

## Size 19-Inch Hat
Continue with All Sizes.

## Size 22-Inch Hat
**Rnd 14:** (Sc in each of next 12 sc, 2 sc in next sc) 6 times. *(84 sc)*

**Rnd 15:** (Sc in ech of next 13 sc, 2 sc in next sc) 6 times. *(90 sc)*

Continue with All Sizes.

## All Sizes
**Rnds 12–25 [14–25, 16–27]:** Sc in each sc around. *(66 [78, 90] sc)*

## Hat Edging

**Rnd 1:** Sl st in next sc, **ch 5** (see Pattern Notes), *sk next sc, **cl** (see Special Stitches) in each of next 2 sc, ch 1, sk next sc, tr in each of next 2 sc, ch 1, rep from * to last 5 sts, sk next st, cl in each of next 2 sc, ch 1, sk next sc, tr in last sc, join in 4th ch of beg ch-5. (22 [26, 30] cls, 22 [22, 30] tr)

**Rnd 2:** Ch 5, *sk next ch-1 sp, **dc dec** (see Special Stitches) in next 2 cls, ch 2, sk next ch-1 sp, dc dec in next 2 tr, ch 2, rep from * to last 2 cls, dc dec in last 2 cls, ch 2, sk next ch-1 sp, join with **joined dc dec** (see Special Stitches) in next tr and in 3rd ch of beg ch-5.

**Rnd 3:** *Picot (see Special Stitches), sc in next ch-2 sp**, sl st in next dc dec, rep from * around, ending last rep at **, join in base of first picot. Fasten off.

## Flower

**Rnd 1:** Ch 3, join in first ch to form ring, ch 1, 5 sc in ring, join in first sc. (5 sc)

**Rnd 2:** *Ch 5, (cl, ch 5, sl st) in same sc as joining, (sl st, ch 5, cl, ch 5, sl st) in each of next 4 sc. Fasten off, leaving an 8-inch tail for sewing. (5 cls, 10 ch-5 sps)

## Finishing

With tapestry needle and yarn tail, sew Flower to Hat. ●

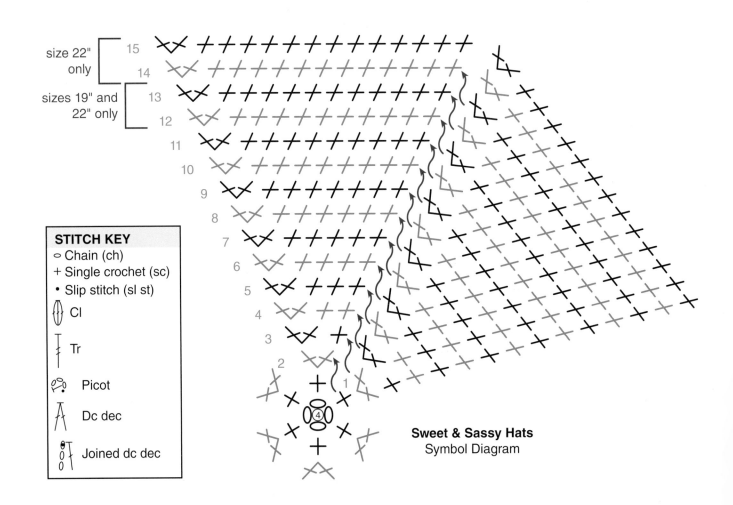

size 22"
only

sizes 19" and
22" only

**STITCH KEY**
- ○ Chain (ch)
- + Single crochet (sc)
- • Slip stitch (sl st)
- Ⓘ Cl
- ╤ Tr
- Picot
- ⋏ Dc dec
- Joined dc dec

**Sweet & Sassy Hats**
Symbol Diagram

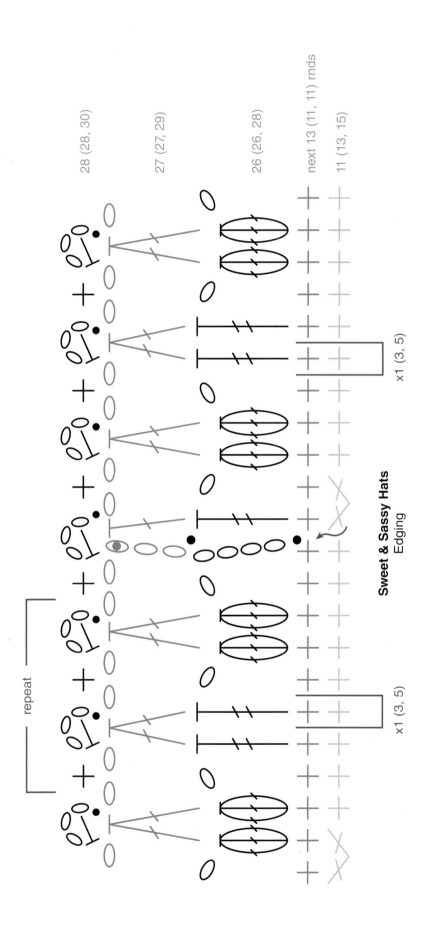

**Sweet & Sassy Hats**
Edging

# Square Motif Blanket

## Skill Level

 **EASY**

## Finished Size

**Baby Blanket:** 38 inches x 38 inches (blocked)

**Throw Blanket:** 53 inches x 53 inches (blocked)

## Materials

- Cascade 220 Heathers medium (worsted) weight yarn (3½ oz/220 yds/100g per hank):
    - 6 hanks #4147 lemon yellow or
    - 12 hanks #9451 Lake Chelan heather
- H/8/5mm crochet hook or size needed to obtain gauge
- Tapestry needle

## Gauge

Rnds 1–5 = 5 inches blocked

Take time to check gauge.

## Pattern Notes

All rounds are worked on right side without turning.

Join with slip stitch as indicated unless otherwise stated.

Motifs are joined together as final round of each is worked.

Chain-3 at beginning of round counts as a double crochet unless otherwise stated.

## First Motif

**Rnd 1:** Ch 5, **join** *(see Pattern Notes)* in first ch from hook to form ring, **ch 3** *(see Pattern Notes)*, 11 dc in ring, join in 3rd (top) ch of beg ch-3. *(12 dc)*

**Rnd 2:** Ch 1, sc in same ch as joining, ch 5, (sc in next st, ch 5) 11 times, join in first sc. *(12 sc, 12 ch-5 sps)*

**Rnd 3:** Sl st in next ch-5 sp, ch 1, sc in same sp, *ch 7 *(corner sp)*, sc in next ch-5 sp, ch 5, sc in next ch-5 sp, ch 5**, sc in next ch-5 sp, rep from * 3 times, ending last rep at **, join in first sc. *(4 ch-7 corner sps, 8 ch-5 sps)*

**Rnd 4:** Sl st in next ch-7 corner sp, ch 3, 8 dc in same corner sp *(beg corner)*, *sc in next ch-5 sp, ch 3, sc in next ch-5 sp**, 9 dc in next ch-7 corner sp *(corner)*, rep from * 3 times, ending last rep at **, join in 3rd ch of beg ch-3. *(4 9-dc corners, 8 sc, 4 ch-3 sps)*

**Rnd 5:** Ch 1, sc in same ch as joining, sc in each of next 3 dc, (sc, ch 7, sc) in next dc *(corner)*, *sc in each of next 4 dc, ch 2, (sc, ch 5, sc) in next ch-3 sp, ch 2**, sc in each of next 4 dc, (sc, ch 7, sc) in next dc *(corner)*, rep from * 3 times, ending last rep at **, join in first sc. Fasten off. *(4 ch-7 corner sps, 4 ch-5 sps)*

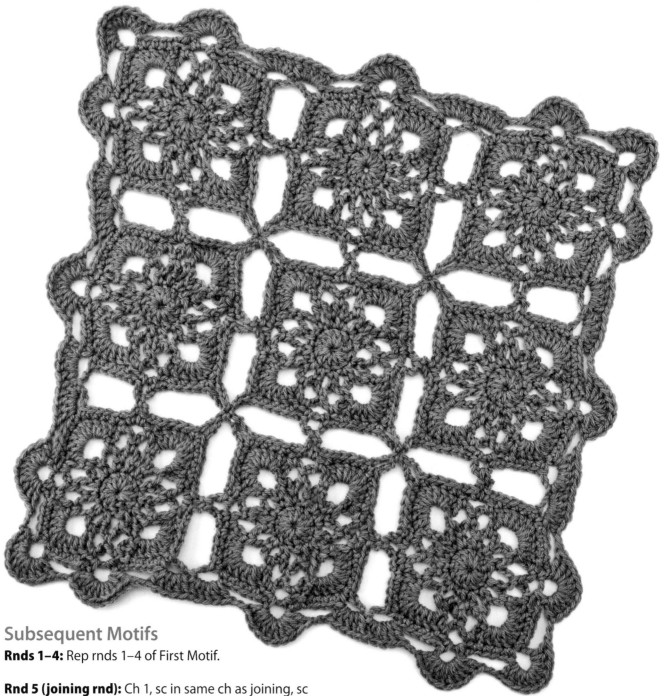

## Subsequent Motifs

**Rnds 1–4:** Rep rnds 1–4 of First Motif.

**Rnd 5 (joining rnd):** Ch 1, sc in same ch as joining, sc in each of next 3 dc, (sc, ch 3, sl st in ch-7 corner sp of adjacent previously made motif, ch 3, sc) in next dc, *sc in each of next 4 dc, ch 2, (sc, ch 2, sl st in ch-5 sp of previously made motif, ch 2, sc) in next ch-5 sp, ch 2**, sc in each of next 4 dc, (sc, ch 7, sc) in next dc, rep from * 3 times, ending last rep at ** and joining where appropriate when matching corners and sides to previous motifs, join in first sc. Fasten off. *(4 ch-7 corner sps, 4 ch-5 sps)*

Continue to join Subsequent Motifs in 7 rows of 7 motifs each for Baby Blanket and 11 rows of 10 motifs each for Throw.

## Edging

Hold piece with RS facing and 1 short end at top, join yarn in ch-7 corner sp in upper right-hand corner, ch 3, 9 dc in same ch-7 sp, *ch 2, 10 dc in next ch-5 sp, ch 2, 5 dc in first ch-7 joined corner, 5 dc in 2nd ch-7 joined corner, rep from * across to next ch-7 corner sp, ch 2, 10 dc in ch-7 corner sp, work in same manner around rem sides, join in 3rd ch of beg ch-3. Fasten off. ●

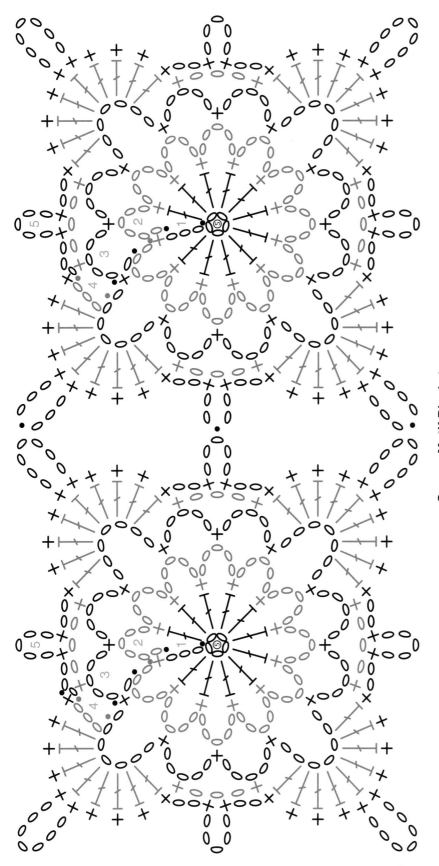

**Square Motif Blanket**
Symbol Diagram

**STITCH KEY**
○ Chain (ch)
+ Single crochet (sc)
• Slip stitch (sl st)
T Double crochet (dc)

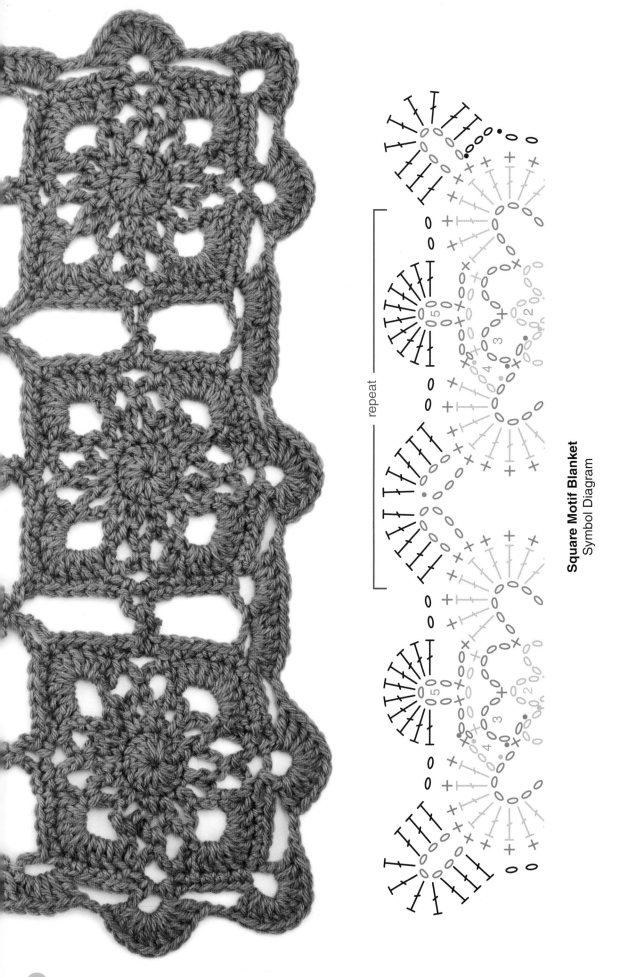

**Square Motif Blanket**
Symbol Diagram

# Shells & Cables Scarf

## Skill Level

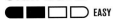 EASY

## Finished Measurements

9½ inches x 64½ inches (blocked, excluding fringe)

## Materials

- Medium (worsted) weight baby alpaca yarn (13/4 oz/125 yds/50g per ball):
    4 balls coral

**3 LIGHT**

- J/10/6mm crochet hook or size needed to obtain gauge
- Tapestry needle

## Gauge

12 sts in pattern = 4 inches; 8 rows in pattern = 4 inches

Take time to check gauge.

## Pattern Notes

Weave in ends as work progresses.

Chain-3 at beginning of row counts as first double crochet unless otherwise stated.

Traditionally keyhole scarves are shorter in total length. You may make either a long keyhole scarf, a short keyhole scarf, or omit keyhole rows and make scarf as long as you like. The pattern is written for a long scarf with a keyhole.

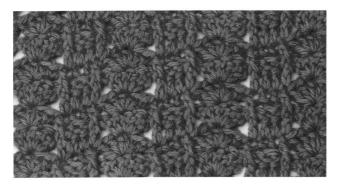

## Special Stitches

**Shell:** 5 dc in indicated st.

**Front post double crochet (fpdc):** Yo, insert hook from front to back and to front again around vertical post (upright part) of indicated st, yo and draw lp through, yo and complete dc.

**Back post double crochet (bpdc):** Yo, insert from back to front to back again around vertical post (upright part) of indicated st, yo and draw lp through, yo and complete dc.

## Scarf

**Row 1 (RS):** Ch 27, sc in 2nd ch from hook, sc in each rem ch across, turn. *(26 sc)*

**Row 2: Ch 3** *(see Pattern Notes)*, *sk next sc, **shell** *(see Special Stitches)* in next sc, sk next sc, dc in each of next 4 sc, rep from * twice, sk next sc, shell in next sc, sk next sc, dc in last sc, turn. *(4 shells, 12 dc)*

**Row 3:** Ch 3, *sk next 2 dc, shell in next dc, sk next 2 dc, **fpdc** *(see Special Stitches)* around next dc, **bpdc** *(see Special Stitches)* around each of next 2 dc, fpdc around next dc, rep from * twice, sk next 2 dc, shell in next dc, sk next 2 dc, dc in last st, turn. *(4 shells, 6 fpdc, 6 bpdc)*

**Row 4:** Ch 3, *sk next 2 dc, shell in next dc, sk next 2 dc, dc in each of next 4 sts, rep from * twice, sk next 2 dc, shell in next dc, sk next 2 dc, dc in last st, turn. *(4 shells, 12 dc)*

**Rows 5–38:** [Rep rows 3 and 4] 17 times.

**Row 39 (keyhole row):** Ch 3, sk next 2 dc, shell in next dc, sk next 2 dc, fpdc around next dc, bpdc around each of next 2 dc, fpdc around next dc, sk next 2 dc, shell in next dc, ch 6 *(keyhole made)*, sk next 8 dc, shell in next dc, sk next 2 dc, fpdc around next dc, bpdc around each of next 2 dc, fpdc around next dc, sk next 2 dc, shell in next dc, sk next 2 dc, dc in last st, turn. *(4 shells, 8 dc, 1 ch-6 sp)*

**Row 40:** Ch 3, sk next 2 dc, shell in next dc, sk next 2 dc, fpdc around next dc, bpdc around each of next 2 dc, fpdc around next dc, sk next 2 dc, shell in next dc, sk next 2 dc, 4 dc in next ch-6 sp, sk next 2 dc, shell in next dc, sk next 2 dc, fpdc around next dc, bpdc around each of next 2 dc, fpdc around next dc, sk next 2 dc, shell in next dc, sk next 2 dc, dc in last st, turn. *(4 shells, 12 dc)*

**Rows 41–108:** [Rep rows 3 and 4] 34 times.

**Row 109:** Rep row 3. Do not fasten off.

## Edging

Ch 1, working in ends of rows across long edge, work 2 sc in end of each dc row, sl st in end of row 1. Fasten off. *(216 sc, 1 sl st)*. Hold piece with rem long side at top and row 1 to right, join with sl st in end of row 1, working in ends of rows across long edge, work 2 sc in each rem row. Fasten off.

## Fringe

Cut 12-inch strands of yarn. For each knot of Fringe, hold 6 strands tog and fold in half. With RS facing and crochet hook, draw folded end from front to back in base of first shell of row 1; draw ends through fold and tighten knot. Tie knots in base of each rem shell of row 1 and in 3rd dc of each shell of row 109. Trim ends even. ●

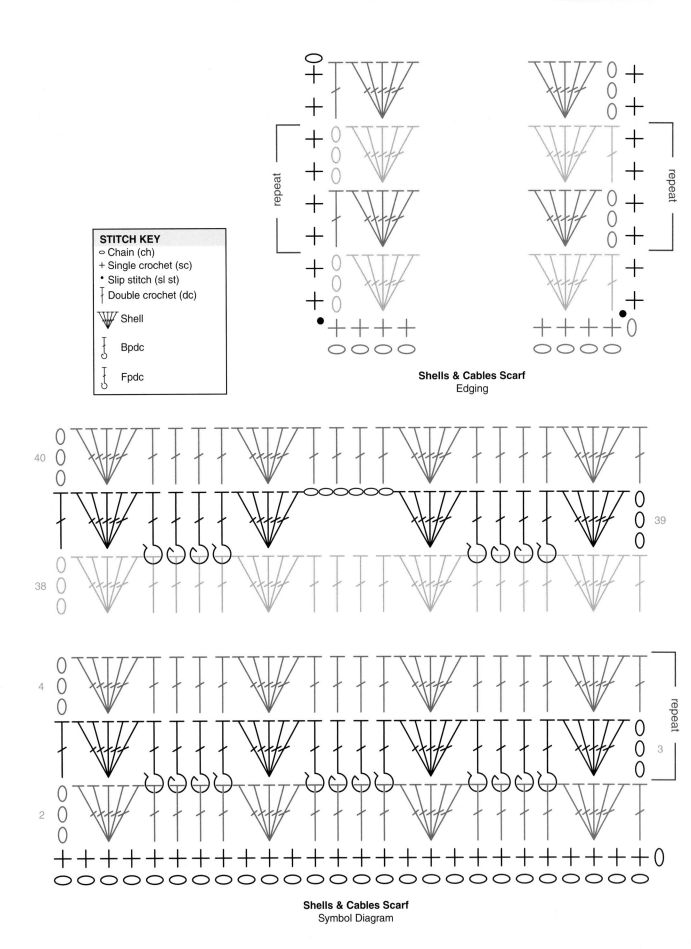

**STITCH KEY**
- ○ Chain (ch)
- + Single crochet (sc)
- • Slip stitch (sl st)
- ╎ Double crochet (dc)
- Shell
- Bpdc
- Fpdc

**Shells & Cables Scarf**
Edging

repeat

40

39

38

4

3

2

**Shells & Cables Scarf**
Symbol Diagram

# STITCH GUIDE

*Need help?* ▶ **StitchGuide.com** • ILLUSTRATED GUIDES • HOW-TO VIDEOS

## STITCH ABBREVIATIONS

| | |
|---|---|
| **beg** | begin/begins/beginning |
| **bpdc** | back post double crochet |
| **bpsc** | back post single crochet |
| **bptr** | back post treble crochet |
| **CC** | contrasting color |
| **ch(s)** | chain(s) |
| **ch-** | refers to chain or space previously made (i.e., ch-1 space) |
| **ch sp(s)** | chain space(s) |
| **cl(s)** | cluster(s) |
| **cm** | centimeter(s) |
| **dc** | double crochet (singular/plural) |
| **dc dec** | double crochet 2 or more stitches together, as indicated |
| **dec** | decrease/decreases/decreasing |
| **dtr** | double treble crochet |
| **ext** | extended |
| **fpdc** | front post double crochet |
| **fpsc** | front post single crochet |
| **fptr** | front post treble crochet |
| **g** | gram(s) |
| **hdc** | half double crochet |
| **hdc dec** | half double crochet 2 or more stitches together, as indicated |
| **inc** | increase/increases/increasing |
| **lp(s)** | loop(s) |
| **MC** | main color |
| **mm** | millimeter(s) |
| **oz** | ounce(s) |
| **pc** | popcorn(s) |
| **rem** | remain/remains/remaining |
| **rep(s)** | repeat(s) |
| **rnd(s)** | round(s) |
| **RS** | right side |
| **sc** | single crochet (singular/plural) |
| **sc dec** | single crochet 2 or more stitches together, as indicated |
| **sk** | skip/skipped/skipping |
| **sl st(s)** | slip stitch(es) |
| **sp(s)** | space(s)/spaced |
| **st(s)** | stitch(es) |
| **tog** | together |
| **tr** | treble crochet |
| **trtr** | triple treble |
| **WS** | wrong side |
| **yd(s)** | yard(s) |
| **yo** | yarn over |

### YARN CONVERSION

| OUNCES TO GRAMS | | GRAMS TO OUNCES | |
|---|---|---|---|
| 1 | 28.4 | 25 | ⅞ |
| 2 | 56.7 | 40 | 1⅔ |
| 3 | 85.0 | 50 | 1¾ |
| 4 | 113.4 | 100 | 3½ |

| UNITED STATES | | UNITED KINGDOM |
|---|---|---|
| sl st (slip stitch) | = | sc (single crochet) |
| sc (single crochet) | = | dc (double crochet) |
| hdc (half double crochet) | = | htr (half treble crochet) |
| dc (double crochet) | = | tr (treble crochet) |
| tr (treble crochet) | = | dtr (double treble crochet) |
| dtr (double treble crochet) | = | ttr (triple treble crochet) |
| skip | = | miss |

**Single crochet decrease (sc dec):** (Insert hook, yo, draw lp through) in each of the sts indicated, yo, draw through all lps on hook.

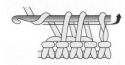

Example of 2-sc dec

**Half double crochet decrease (hdc dec):** (Yo, insert hook, yo, draw lp through) in each of the sts indicated, yo, draw through all lps on hook.

Example of 2-hdc dec

**Reverse single crochet (reverse sc):** Ch 1, sk first st, working from left to right, insert hook in next st from front to back, draw up lp on hook, yo and draw through both lps on hook.

**Chain (ch):** Yo, pull through lp on hook.

**Single crochet (sc):** Insert hook in st, yo, pull through st, yo, pull through both lps on hook.

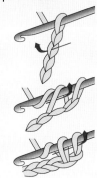

**Double crochet (dc):** Yo, insert hook in st, yo, pull through st, [yo, pull through 2 lps] twice.

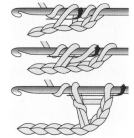

**Double crochet decrease (dc dec):** (Yo, insert hook, yo, draw lp through, yo, draw through 2 lps on hook) in each of the sts indicated, yo, draw through all lps on hook.

Example of 2-dc dec

**Front loop (front lp) Back loop (back lp)**

Front Loop   Back Loop

**Front post stitch (fp): Back post stitch (bp):** When working post st, insert hook from right to left around post of st on previous row.

Back   Front

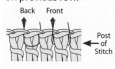

Post of Stitch

**Half double crochet (hdc):** Yo, insert hook in st, yo, pull through st, yo, pull through all 3 lps on hook.

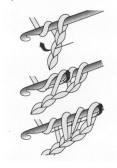

**Double treble crochet (dtr):** Yo 3 times, insert hook in st, yo, pull through st, [yo, pull through 2 lps] 4 times.

**Treble crochet decrease (tr dec):** Holding back last lp of each st, tr in each of the sts indicated, yo, pull through all lps on hook.

Example of 2-tr dec

**Slip stitch (sl st):** Insert hook in st, pull through both lps on hook.

**Chain color change (ch color change)** Yo with new color, draw through last lp on hook.

**Double crochet color change (dc color change)** Drop first color, yo with new color, draw through last 2 lps of st.

**Treble crochet (tr):** Yo twice, insert hook in st, yo, pull through st, [yo, pull through 2 lps] 3 times.

*Annie's*®    *Learn to Crochet* is published by Annie's, 306 East Parr Road, Berne, IN 46711. Printed in USA. Copyright © 2014, 2016 Annie's. All rights reserved. This publication may not be reproduced in part or in whole without written permission from the publisher.

**RETAIL STORES:** If you would like to carry this pattern book or any other Annie's publication, visit AnniesWSL.com.

ISBN: 978-1-57367-486-7

3 4 5 6 7 8 9

Today is the day you learn how to crochet and discover a relaxing hobby you'll enjoy for life! Join crochet instructor Ellen Gormley as she makes learning how to crochet fun and easy. In this video class from Annie's, Ellen demonstrates how to crochet all the basic stitches for both right- and left-handers!

## DVD Includes:

- All the basics of crochet, including how to hold the yarn and crochet hook, types of yarns, hooks and basic notions.
- Basic stitches, including chain, slip stitch, single crochet, half-double crochet, double crochet, treble crochet, shells, clusters and post stitches.
- How to work in rows and rounds.
- How to increase and decrease.
- How to crochet a basic motif for creating a baby blanket or afghan.
- DVDs are compatible with North American DVD players, and PC and Macintosh computer systems.

## Book Includes:

- Instructions for 5 easy patterns to help you practice what you have learned. (Patterns are not included on the DVD.)

U.S. $19.99 CANADA $23.99     ISBN: 978-1-57367-486-7

UPC 7 32526 40994 3
EAN 9 781573 674867
5 1999

PRINTED IN USA
AnniesCatalog.com

| LANGUAGE | English | COLOR | Dual Layer |
|---|---|---|---|
| CAPTIONS SUBTITLES | CC Captioned | Subtitles | 3 Hr. 3 Mins. |

**SYSTEM REQUIREMENTS**
To view the class DVD, use a television with a DVD player or a computer manufactured in the past few years with a DVD-ROM drive and appropriate DVD player software. To view the pattern CD, a computer with the current version of the free Adobe® Reader® available from www.adobe.com is required.